Pebble Plus
Bilingüe/Bilingual

Cómo hacer un cohete efervescente
How to Build a Fizzy Rocket

A divertirse con la ciencia
Hands-On Science Fun

por/by Lori Shores

Editora consultora/Consulting Editor: Gail Saunders-Smith, PhD

Consultor/Consultant: Ronald Browne, PhD
Departamento de Educación Elemental y de Primera Infancia/
Department of Elementary & Early Childhood Education
Universidad Estatal de Minnesota, Mankato/Minnesota State University, Mankato

CAPSTONE PRESS
a capstone imprint

Pebble Plus is published by Capstone Press,
151 Good Counsel Drive, P.O. Box 669, Mankato, Minnesota 56002.
www.capstonepub.com

 Books published by Capstone Press are manufactured with paper
containing at least 10 percent post-consumer waste.

Library of Congress Cataloging-in-Publication Data
Shores, Lori.
  [How to build a fizzy rocket. Spanish & English]
  Como hacer un cohete efervescente / por Lori Shores = How to build a fizzy rocket / by Lori Shores.
     p. cm.—(Pebble plus bilingüe. A divertirse con la ciencia = Pebble plus bilingual. Hands-on science fun)
  Includes bibliographical references and index.
  Summary: "Simple text and full-color photos instruct readers how to build a fizzy rocket and explains the science
behind the activity—in both English and Spanish"—Provided by publisher.
  ISBN 978-1-4296-6105-8 (library binding)
  1. Rockets (Aeronautics)—Models—Juvenile literature. I. Title. II. Title: How to build a fizzy rocket.
  TL844.S5618 2011
  621.43'560228—dc22   2010042261

Editorial Credits
Erika L. Shores, editor; Strictly Spanish, translation services; Juliette Peters, designer; Danielle Ceminsky, bilingual
   book designer; Sarah Schuette; photo studio specialist; Marcy Morin, scheduler; Laura Manthe, production specialist

Photo Credits
Capstone Studio/Karon Dubke, all

Artistic Effects: iStockphoto/solos, cover, 1, 2, 3, 22, 23, 24 (starfield design); Otto Rogge Photography, 4-5 (clouds)

Safety Note/Nota de seguridad

Please ask an adult for help in building and launching your fizzy rocket./
Pídele a un adulto que te ayude a hacer y lanzar tu cohete efervescente.

Note to Parents and Teachers

The A divertirse con la ciencia/Hands-On Science Fun set supports national science standards
related to physical science. This book describes and illustrates building a fizzy rocket in both
English and Spanish. The images support early readers in understanding the text. The repetition
of words and phrases helps early readers learn new words. This book also introduces early
readers to subject-specific vocabulary words, which are defined in the Glossary section. Early
readers may need assistance to read some words and to use the Table of Contents, Glossary,
Internet Sites, and Index sections of the book.

Printed in the United States of America in North Mankato, Minnesota.
092010   005933CGS11

Table of Contents

Getting Started 4

Making a Fizzy Rocket 6

How Does It Work? 18

Glossary 22

Internet Sites 22

Index 24

Tabla de contenidos

Para empezar 4

Cómo hacer un cohete efervescente . 6

¿Cómo funciona? 18

Glosario 23

Sitios de Internet 23

Índice 24

Getting Started

Rockets blast off into space.
You can use simple materials
to launch your own rocket
into the air.

Para empezar

Los cohetes viajan al espacio a
grandes velocidades. Tú puedes
usar materiales sencillos para
lanzar tu propio cohete al aire.

Here's what you need/Necesitarás:

tape/cinta

scissors/tijeras

8.5″ x 11″ (22 cm x 28 cm)
sheet of paper/hoja de papel

safety glasses/
lentes de seguridad

white plastic film canister
with a lid that fits inside/
bote blanco de plástico para
película fotográfica con una
tapa que quepa dentro

½ of a fizzing antacid
tablet made with
sodium bicarbonate/
½ tableta efervescente
de antiácido de
bicarbonato de sodio

1 teaspoon (5 mL) warm water/
1 cucharadita (5 ml) de agua tibia

Making a Fizzy Rocket

Cut the paper in half.

One half will be the body
of the rocket.

Cómo hacer un cohete efervescente

Corta la hoja de papel a la mitad.

Una mitad será el cuerpo
del cohete.

6

Tape the edge of the paper to the upside-down film canister.

Form the paper into a tube.

Tape down the other edge of paper.

Pega con cinta la orilla del papel al bote de plástico con la parte abierta hacia abajo.

Forma un tubo con el papel.

Pega con cinta la otra orilla del papel.

9

Cut a circle from the other half of paper.

Cut a slit, and overlap the sides to form a cone.

Tape the cone on top of the tube.

Cut out two triangles, and tape them to the tube for fins.

Recorta un círculo de la otra mitad del papel. Corta una ranura y empalma los lados para formar un cono. Pega con cinta el cono a la parte superior del tubo.

Recorta dos triángulos y pégalos con cinta al tubo para formar las aletas.

Put on safety glasses,
and turn over the rocket.

Then add 1 teaspoon (5 mL)
of warm water to the canister.

Ponte los lentes de seguridad y
da vuelta el cohete.

Añade 1 cucharadita (5 ml) de
agua tibia al bote.

Take the rocket, lid, and antacid outside.

Drop the half tablet of antacid
into the water.

Snap the lid on right away.

Lleva afuera el cohete, la tapa y
la tableta efervescente.

Pon la media tableta de antiácido
en el agua.

Coloca de inmediato la tapa.

Quickly stand up the rocket.

Step back about 6 feet (2 meters)
to watch.

How high will the rocket go?

Para el cohete rápidamente.

Retírate unos 6 pies (2 metros)
para observar.

¿Qué tan alto subirá el cohete?

How Does It Work?

A reaction started when the antacid tablet and water mixed. The water and the tablet made little bubbles of gas.

¿Cómo funciona?

Una reacción se inició cuando se mezclaron la tableta de antiácido y el agua. El agua y la tableta formaron pequeñas burbujas de gas.

gas bubbles/
burbujas de gas

Soon the canister filled with gas. Pressure inside the canister made the lid pop off. As gas rushed out, the canister was pushed into the air.

Muy pronto el bote se llenó de gas. La presión dentro del bote hizo que la tapa se separara. Al salir rápidamente el gas, el bote salió disparado en el aire.

21

Glossary

antacid—a medicine that reduces the amount of acid in your stomach to soothe an upset stomach

fin—a small, triangular structure on a rocket used to help with steering

gas—a substance, such as air, that spreads to fill any space that holds it

launch—to send a rocket into space

material—the thing from which something is made

pressure—a force made by pressing on something

reaction—an action in response to something that happens

Internet Sites

FactHound offers a safe, fun way to find Internet sites related to this book. All of the sites on FactHound have been researched by our staff.

Here's all you do:

Visit *www.facthound.com*

Type in this code: 9781429661058

Super-cool stuff!

Check out projects, games and lots more at
www.capstonekids.com

Glosario

la aleta—una pequeña estructura triangular en un cohete que se usa para ayudar a dirigirlo

el antiácido—una medicina que reduce la cantidad de ácido del estómago para aliviar el malestar estomacal

el gas—una sustancia, como el aire, que se extiende para llenar cualquier espacio que la contenga

lanzar—enviar un cohete al espacio

el material—de lo que está hecho algo

la presión—una fuerza hecha al presionar algo

la reacción—una acción en respuesta a algo que ocurre

Sitios de Internet

FactHound brinda una forma segura y divertida de encontrar sitios de Internet relacionados con este libro. Todos los sitios en FactHound han sido investigados por nuestro personal.

Esto es todo lo que tienes que hacer:

Visita *www.facthound.com*

Ingresa este código: 978142961058

¡Algo súper divertido! Hay proyectos, juegos y mucho más en www.capstonekids.com

Index

air, 4, 20

antacids, 5, 14, 18

bubbles, 18

cone, 10

film canisters, 5, 8,
    12, 20

fins, 10

gas, 18, 20

launch, 4, 16

lids, 5, 14, 20

pressure, 20

reaction, 18

safety glasses, 5, 12

tube, 8, 10

water, 5, 12, 14, 18

Índice

agua, 5, 12, 14, 18

aire, 4, 20

aletas, 10

antiácidos, 5, 14, 18

bote para película, 5, 8,
    12, 20

burbujas, 18

cono, 10

gas, 18, 20

lanzar, 4, 16

lentes de seguridad, 5, 12

presión, 20

reacción, 18

tapas, 5, 14, 20

tubo, 8, 10